Think Positive

How to Be More Positive and Attract Happiness

by William Talbot

Table of Contents

Introduction

Cynics often refer to positive people as naïve. Yet nothing could be further from the truth. Positivity isn't the denial of reality, but rather it's about accepting the fact that both good and bad experiences are an essential part of life, and thereby choosing not to spend time dwelling over adversities and misfortunes. Therefore, positive people actively choose to follow the paths which allow them to bring more good into their lives, even in the midst of otherwise negative situations.

While the understanding of positivity may have begun by classifying it as a coping mechanism, this view is widely regarded by psychologists as an overly simplistic and narrow-minded one. Instead, positivity is a way of life which allows its practitioners to live more satisfying, healthier, and longer lives. And none of those qualifiers are an exaggeration.

Positive people are 80% less likely to suffer from stress management or anxiety disorders right off the bat. Moreover, they're less prone to cardiovascular diseases, and have better motivational drive and energy than their counterparts. Though running around in a constant state of panic from excessive attention on the negative may professionally incite some people to work harder and try to be better in some way or another, it makes for a pretty short life — successful as it may be. In the end, the "positives" always pull out ahead over diehard "realists" and pessimists who refuse to let go of the bad in their lives.

With all this in mind, people often wonder whether positivity is an attribute which can be consciously inculcated into one's life. And the answer is: Yes! A *resounding* **Yes**! But we'll discuss this further in the subsequent chapters.

So, while positivity isn't a magic key that unlocks a lifetime full of glitter and candy, it certainly *does* allow you to appreciate everything great about life. It even allows you to maintain your calm and composure so that you can actively navigate your way to happier times on your own merit. And the good news is, believe it or not, being positive isn't nearly as hard as it seems. I'm going to help open up your mind to bringing about some simple internal and external changes that are guaranteed to bring greater peace, happiness, and fulfillment into your life. So, if you're ready to learn the secrets of positivity and how to adopt a more positive perspective on life, then let's get started!

Chapter 1: The Fundamentals of Positivity

As I mentioned earlier, positivity isn't about putting on blinders and ignoring the downsides of one's life or circumstances. Rather, it's an active effort to identify, understand, and appreciate all the good in it. Often, in periods of trouble or high stress, it becomes altogether too easy to forget all the blessings and boons, all the joys and the great people around who share in it, and all the fruits of hard work and planning which have afforded a person their current state of happiness in life. Instead, the 60% of good in one's life—made up through one's dream job or academic path, one's relative financial comfort, great state of physical health, or even just the awesome friends and family around—are ignored, while the petty troubles, squabbles, and obstacles are blown increasingly out of proportion till they're all that's visible in one's perspective.

Positivity doesn't let you forget those big or small problems. It doesn't tell you that life is a dream woven from rainbows, where unicorns are household pets, and leprechauns run around showering households with gold. Instead, it calms you down with a nice warm glass of milk and a delicious cookie, and tells you that no matter how bad things may seem to be, we have all the skills and tools we need to solve the problem at hand. And as I said, this is an entirely active and conscious choice. You *can* choose to keep wallowing in negativity and self-pity, just like you *can* choose to spray itching powder in your underwear right before heading out to the office—but why would you?

Now, while there may be ridiculously positive people on earth who make it all seem so simple, yet simultaneously difficult if you aren't born that way; for most "positives", it was a matter of inducing positivity through conscious effort in their routine till it became an automatic way of thinking. And that took time and dedication. But, knowing the benefits of positivity, I'd say that's still a pretty sweet deal, wouldn't you?

But, there are prerequisites if you wish to induce positivity within you as an attribute. As you must have understood, positivity cannot exist in a state of self-denial—that's called naiveté, and that's a whole *other* brand of dangerous and stupid self-harm. Therefore, the very first thing which you need to do before we move on is to accept the harsh realities of your life, difficult as they may be. And I don't want to hear

"But that's what I think about day and night. Why else would I pick up this book?" I don't mean thinking about the problems you face, while denying them in reality. I don't even mean sitting and stewing in them, while denying any physical reality or actuality to them by refusing to utter them out loud.

So, take a seat in a comfortable and safe environment, when you're all by yourself, and say each problem that plagues you out loud. Problems at the office? List them out to yourself. Feeling unsatisfied in your relationship, or don't feel like your studies are going as well as you hoped? Blurt them out, exactly as you happen to think of them. Go on, finish this exercise while I wait for you.

While you're at it, also mention everything in life that usually gets you down—your deepest fears, your biggest disappointments, your usual insecurities. You *know* that you have a negative outlook on life and yourself, and you admitted it the moment you picked up this book. It wasn't just an idle curiosity, or any of the other excuses which you've offered up at the altar of your self-denial till this point. And yes, I know you hate being told how you feel—but it's still true. So, do yourself a favor, and admit everything that you believe contributes to your mentality of negativity. If

9

you have trust issues that can be traced back to issues with your childhood or even a former partner—admit them to yourself, along with why you feel that way, and throw in a couple of cuss-words at those responsible for good measure. Why not? You *are* by yourself after all. And if you can't be honest even with yourself about the way you feel, how do you ever expect to pull yourself out of negativity. "It's darkest before dawn" and all that, after all.

Only once you admit the truth of every single problem, ill-thought, worry, fear, insecurity, and other negative emotions and feelings anchoring you down, at least to yourself *out loud,* can you hope to start making some meaningful changes in your life and your way of living. People often fear that saying things out loud gives them more physical substance, and hence more power to do damage to themselves. The reality is quite contrary to that. It's the *fear* we attach to them, which gives them power—not saying it out loud. Just like people refused to say *Voldemort,* and kept on referring to the evil snake-wizard from *Harry Potter* as "You-Know-Who", like giggling teens talking about Sarah's crush right before prom.

So, ditch that baggage of fear, and revel in the awesome empowering sensation of being entirely honest with yourself, for the first time I might add. And once that's done, take the next step, and move on to the second chapter.

Chapter 2: Setting the Baseline

Once you've admitted the negative realities of your situation to yourself, it's time to move on and set the foundation for positivity. Now, positivity is difficult to achieve in a mind which is easily shaken by problems and minor issues. That's because people who freak out over anything and everything rarely have the presence of mind and composure to actually analyze a situation and understand *just how much worse things could have realistically been.* It's like the sophomore in horror movies who *always* gets killed first. Unlike the protagonist of the movie, who takes action when necessary, assesses the resources at hand when required, and plans ways out of the situation when time is available, the sophomore just keeps flailing her arms and running around panicking like a headless chicken.

As clichéd as this suggestion may be, the best way to create a frame of mind which can house positivity is through meditation. While it has several other mental and physical benefits, the most important thing which yoga and other meditative forms teach you is to completely immerse yourself in the moment and forget everything else that's happening around you. One of the best forms of meditative techniques which promote calm and composure, among the burgeoning multitudes available, is mindfulness.

Now, this technique is widely used in several forms of Buddhism as a method of attaining enlightenment. But, at its very base, mindfulness refers to a state where you're *mindful* or paying attention to yourself in the very moment when you're performing it. So, choose a comfortable corner of your house or your bedroom—one which makes you feel safe and relaxed. You don't need to sit in meditative positions, sit or lie down however you like. However, if you're lying down, do so on your back, with your arms and legs comfortably outstretched outwards with the palms of your hands facing upwards. If you're sitting, keep your hands comfortably on your lap or knees, again with the palms facing upwards. If you wish, you can play some nature sounds or quiet, soothing, instrumental music in the background as well.

Once you're comfortable, simply start breathing in and out deeply, letting your belly expand when you breathe in and deflate when you breathe out. Once you've established a regular rhythm (one way of doing so is breathing in to a count of 5, holding your breath till a count of 2, and then breathing out to a count of 5), start paying attention to the way your body feels in that moment. Reflect on the way your lungs feel each time you breathe in and out, or the way your stomach feels each time it expands. Then move outwards to your hands and feet. Without moving, try to sense the way your fingers and toes feel in the moment—and attempt to sense the rush of blood to and back from your limbs. Each time some other thought or worry or urgency towards some work which needs to be done tries to intrude upon your quiet moment, push it gently away. Tell yourself that there's absolutely nothing in the world which would change if the worry or task at hand were entertained a few minutes later rather than right that very second.

After you've done this for a while, get up and get back to your normal schedule—but don't rush. Take a casual pace. You won't be early or late to get to anything, you'll reach right on time for whatever needs to be done. Saving up 30 seconds by throwing yourself into a state of panic will achieve nothing but stress for yourself in the long run.

After you've done this, at any point of time in the day available to you during your schedule, for a few days at the very least, it's time to move on to focused meditation. This basically involves the same process, but includes a chant as well. Now, while the usual

15

chant is "Om" based on Sanskrit traditions in Yoga and meditation, you can use pretty much anything you like. The only characteristic, which it needs to fulfill, is that it should be short. I mean, you can't really chant "supercalifragilisticexpialidocious", can you? So, it can either be something short and meaningful or short and pointless. You could even sit and chant "Spoon" if you like—though the word will lose all meaning after about 40 repetitions. But that just makes it more amusing. Or you can choose "Confidence" or even "Calm". These last two are particularly powerful, by the way.

Anyway, in the same manner as the first meditative set, follow the exact routine but add the chant every time you breathe out—instead of just simply breathing out. Keep repeating the chant over and over, till you're saying it on autopilot. Focus only on saying the chant out loud, but let your mind travel inwards and *feel* your body each time you utter the word. Pay attention to the way your throat and mouth shape words, or even the sensation in your chest as you intone it out loud. In this manner, you will slowly learn to reduce the intense urgency and panic arising from any problems which may crop up—and that's an important foundation to set. After about a week of this practice, you'll automatically find yourself more willing to analyze a situation calmly instead of jumping to the worst conclusion from the get-go, as you once did.

One last activity, which can work wonders for this foundation, is exercise. While this may again be another dead horse which has been flogged around for far too long, it works for a very simple reason— endorphins. Positivity is far easier to achieve when you aren't always feeling like a piece of used chewing gum that's been stuck under the study desk for far too long, and nothing helps with that like nature's own Super Prozac. Not only that, but also endorphins aside, the bid to get physically fitter may also help you deal with some deeper insecurities rising out of your self-image. The world becomes much prettier as a place to live in when you feel attractive.

Once you've completed these conditions, and believe that you're finally starting to calm down and compose yourself better than you did before—pat yourself on the back. You've just finished laying an incredibly important yet difficult foundation. In essence, you've created your baseline for positivity. Since positivity isn't the absence of negativity, but active ways of denying the latter any power or control over one's thought and satisfaction from life, the strength of this baseline will determine how effectively you launch

17

yourself into the stratosphere of "positives" from here on out.

Chapter 3: Making Changes on the Inside

Now, if you were living in the trashiest neighborhood there ever was, and were given unlimited resources, time, and manpower to clean it all up, with enough incentives to harden your resolve—where would you start? You certainly wouldn't start from the furthest point away from your house and work backwards, would you? Certainly not. You'd start from your own house and backyard, and then work outwards from there. In the same manner, if you wish to combat negativity in your life, you need to first start with yourself.

The very first move on your part in this battle will be to start policing your thoughts. More often than not, we are the largest perpetrators of negativity within ourselves. This means that if you're ever to break out of this cycle, you need to be your own warden, and make sure that you control your mind and not the other way round. If the idea of controlling your own mind sounds silly, it's because your head can't accurately separate the idea of your collective thoughts and experiences embodied within your head from your innate sense of *self*. Your mind, and who you are as a person are entirely separate concepts.

This is why people are rarely entirely logical about their actions and choices, because those are dictated by something far more tightly intertwined with who we are than the neurotic bundle of reasoning we call our brain.

So, whenever you feel as if you're being too negative—either to yourself, or to others around you—you need to cut yourself off right away, and change your thought to one with more optimism or positivity. And this is going to be extremely difficult. If you feel as if you're letting your trust issues get in the way of giving someone you barely know the benefit of the doubt, no matter how well justified, change your stance from veiled hostility or neutrality to *slight* optimism—not so much as to get hurt if you're wrong, but enough to not spoil *your* day or mood. The entire point of this scenario would be that if you *have* to deal with people not worth your time, blind trust would just hurt you and blind distrust would just spoil your mood and day anyway. Therefore, as long as they aren't harming you in any way *right now*, don't treat them the way you think they should be *right now* either. As we discussed, being positive isn't the same as being naive, it's knowing how to make the best out of a bad situation.

If you feel as if your insecurities are holding you back from trying a new experience, or enjoying something which you would have participated in had you had more confidence, go give it a shot—even if only to see if you were right. However, do this *each* time to see if you're right *each* time. Don't just try something once and walk away, shaking your head and mumbling, "Yup, I was right." I promise you—if you try this enough times, you *will* be proved wrong far more often than not.

The second thing, which you need to do, is to *accurately* assess your options. The biggest problem with people plagued by negativity is that they're adamant about sticking with worst-case scenarios in every situation. Now, if this meant that they would be pleasantly surprised thanks to their negative expectations when something good came along, the world would be much simpler and happier as a place. However, even when something good *does* come along, "negatives" are hell-bent on dissecting it down till they can see the downsides, just so that they can go, "Aha! I was right!" And for all of those who just went "Bull$%#*! You think I like being so negative all the time? You think I do this to myself?" No, you definitely don't *like* it, but you **do** do this to yourself.

So, what you need to do is to open your eyes and look at the reality of situations which keep hiding in that massive blind spot of yours. There are *very* few situations in the world which are bad in every way—and most of them involve some baddie holding a gun to your head, or locking you up in a basement. Aside from such scenarios, every other thing, which has ever happened to you and *will* ever happen to you, will *always* carry at least some good with the bad, if only you're clear-headed enough to be able to see it.

Therefore, whenever a set of choices, or a situation, or a problem happens to present itself to you, first take a breath before you act, and try to look at it from as many angles as possible. Worried about next month's rent? Well, you were thinking about a second job anyway to save up for that trip in winter. And this will give you more drive and force to go after it aggressively. Also, you have almost an entire month to come up with a solution, and that should be ample time to find a solution if you pour your heart and soul into it. This way, such a problem could potentially unlock the way to future stability and give you the kick you need to pursue that second job. It may have been worrisome, but there are definitely lots of choices in your hands, and you *can* make something out of them, if only you would stop wallowing and sulking in the face of tribulations.

In this manner, use your head to accurately and comprehensively uncover all your options and choices in any given scenario. If you feel trapped or stuck, it's only because you haven't taken the time to think of more solutions yet, even when some may have occurred to you. And once you know how to deal with yourself, it's time you learned how to deal with others to create positivity.

Chapter 4: Making Changes on the Outside

After having dealt with your head, it's time to address your environment. All ancient traditions, without a single exception, treat positive outlooks which must not only be generated through one's own conscious thought but also through the manipulation of positive energy in one's environment. The fallout from not doing so is to physically and mentally stagnate in malignant, static, or polluted energies. Now, while I may not know much about "energies", I do know this—nothing causes a negative outlook more than a dirty environment.

So, always make sure that your surroundings are clean and organized. This will reduce chaos around your household life, and prevent frustration and other negative frames of mind. Even though I'm well aware that this step will be burdensome to some of you, and that others may perform better when working in their own chaotic environment, your productivity doesn't change if you clean and clear up *after* you're done with something. Moreover, by putting in that effort yourself and basking in the *positive* results from it, it would become harder for your life to not feel lighter and brighter.

And that's the next thing—even if your surroundings are clean, it won't help your state of mind if they're too austere or depressing. Therefore, add more color to your surroundings, even if only in the form of the bedsheets which you sleep on every night. Moreover, get yourself some inspirational posters and put them up on walls where they would be the first thing to catch your eye every morning. They don't have to be Hallmark cheesy, and you can easily select bright ones with pictures and messages that personally appeal to you if you search for them with some dedication. However, remove any paintings, posters, drapes, sheets, etc., which are too dark and simply add gloom to your household—regardless of how chic they may appear to be. Once you're positive enough to not need this book anymore, you can bring them back. Till then, I'm trying to help you, so you better listen.

Another step which you may find difficult to follow is this—get yourself new and colorful clothes. Again, you don't need to look like you stole a pimp's apparel. However, they do need to be brighter colors which seem soothing or exciting to you. If you do already wear such clothes, ditch those and buy new ones. Try fresh colors for good measure, since the last ones were obviously not helping.

The final step, which you may need to take, is this—identify people who instigate your negative thoughts or even feed them, and cut them out of your life. This is going to be extremely difficult, and you'll find yourself making rationalizations and excuses on their behalf, but it's still necessary beyond all doubt. And if you feel particularly negative, especially about yourself or your capability to handle problems, you definitely have *some* of them around even if you can't identify them at first. The easiest way to be able to recognize such people is by separating those who make you feel worse about yourself in any way after you interact with them. Now, in some cases, that person may be a colleague or an employer, and you can't cut off contact with them—but you can reduce it till you're strong enough to stand up for yourself.

Whether the people in question are members of your family, peers at academic institutions, or even friends and acquaintances, such people may often create dependence on them by first making you feel bad or inadequate and then supporting you through that feeling or offering you their own metaphorical shoulder upon which to cry. Such folks are reservoirs of insidious toxicity in people's lives, and are often directly responsible for amplifying or directly feeding large quantities of negativity held inside you. They need to be cut out—preferably permanently, but at least temporarily so, if the first option isn't possible.

Chapter 5: Daily Positivity Exercises

Once the steps covered in Chapters 1 through 4 are finished, it's time to start building your daily reservoir of positivity. While meditation and exercise will help you feel better about yourself, the exercises from Chapter 3 will help reduce the creation and perpetuation of negativity, and Chapter 4 will work on that foundation to build it into positive reminders, these exercises will help you fill your reservoir of positivity with good and vibrant energy. Also, It will help you appreciate the small ways in which positivity can grow and spread. While I have three exercises which you must fulfill every day, the first two among them need to be completed at least once a day, while the last one must be satisfied whenever and however often the opportunity presents itself.

The first of these exercises must be completed before you go to sleep and must continue right when you wake up and get out of bed. Whether under your mattress, or by your bedside, start keeping a tiny notebook, pad, post-it stand, whatever, along with a full glass of water. When you're in bed, whether you fall asleep while watching something or just lie down naturally and drift off—as soon as you close your eyes, push a big smile on your face, take a deep breath while smiling, and then go to sleep. Even if you feel like warmed-up boogers, force that smile on your face. You're going to sleep in a safe environment, regardless of whether it's comfortable or not—things could easily be worse. Never go to bed angry or upset, even if you feel horrid and are entirely faking the smile, and you've won half the battle.

As soon as you wake up, stretch and gulp down the water. When you're drinking it, imagine the clean water entering your body and purifying any negative energy or thoughts which you may have accumulated during the night through nightmares, errant thoughts, etc. Once you go to the restroom, imagine you're getting rid of all that negativity through the toxins leaving your body. As awkward as this description may seem right now, if you don't believe that's effective, try it for a few days. I guarantee that this thought process will become quite addictive soon enough. After having drunk the water, and before you entirely get out of "sleepy-mode", get that pad or whatever, and write one good thing about yourself. It could be that you love the way your hair looks that day, or that your eyes seem sparklier than usual, or even general stuff like you're far more intelligent, capable, or good-looking than others, or play chess better than others around you, etc. Whatever you do, do not continue with your day till you've written down one good thing about yourself.

The second of these exercises is to find some time each day when you can talk—to yourself. If you find that your mood drops towards negativity during afternoons or evenings, schedule 15 minutes for yourself accordingly. When you sit down for this talk, first tell yourself that you're capable of facing any problem that comes your way, then list one thing about your day so far where you were either really happy or really impressed with yourself. Don't discount this exercise as foolish or childish. The bravest of men and women charging into battle often give themselves a quick pep-talk before dashing out of cover—everyone needs to pick themselves up on a regular basis over something or the other. So, don't denigrate this measure, utilize it honestly as a tool to remind yourself of how great you are.

If your negativity doesn't arise from yourself, but rather problems like trust issues when dealing with others around you, take this time to list one thing that other people did which made you happy and slightly more willing to trust them. Or something that they did that impressed or surprised you in a good way. Or made you feel closer to them. Or even just made you feel appreciated.

And now we come to the last of these daily exercises—practicing gratitude. Now, while this may seem rather small, that's exactly why it's so effective. Gratitude is something so insignificant in daily life that we feel a bland "Thank you" with no emotions behind it covers our side of the interaction. However, since it's so insignificant, it loses all meaning, and the world is deprived of a truly positive experience.

So, if someone does anything for you at all—from the tiniest of actions to something big and memorable— allow yourself to actually *feel* a tinge of true gratitude towards them. Even if the action in question is as basic a part of social etiquette as letting you walk through a door first if you're a female, don't write it off simply as something which was supposed to be done and so you don't owe anyone anything beyond an emotionless "Thanks". Or even if you're living with your parent(s), and your mum or dad take the time to wake you up in the morning even when they're in a desperate rush.

Whenever someone does absolutely anything for you, appreciate them for doing something which they needn't have under any circumstance, and only did out of consideration for you—and allow yourself to *feel* that sense of gratitude. Not a sense of obligation

34

to someone, but a simple feeling of having received someone else's efforts and thoughts with the aim of improving your life even if in the smallest ways possible. Then allow that feeling to grow into a vibrant smile, don't be an arrogant douche about it, and thank them from the bottom of your heart. Do the same even if you're taking part in a transaction, and are paying someone for a service.

This will create a sense of conscious gratitude, in which you allow the positivity of that moment to reflect and amplify within you, and then send that positivity back to the person who started the cycle through their efforts. Do this simple thing, and they will gladly put in any effort for you. Do this at your usual bagel or coffee stand, and the seller will always greet you with a smile from then on. Give positivity to receive positivity, and there are few simpler ways to embed this sense in your life.

Conclusion

People often make a big deal out of positivity, but the fact is that most of us have just forgotten how to understand and appreciate life's smaller pleasures. Since most of us are perpetually embroiled in the needs of the ever-present rat race, we lose sight of the fact that—unless you're homeless in a famine-wrought land, without any family or loved ones, and are destined to die in the next hour—there are plenty of things to be thankful for. And positivity is hard to deny or keep out of one's mentality once that realization becomes clear.

As we mentioned before, once you accept the reality of your situation, try to look at the bright side of it, and direct your actions to get whatever favorable outcome you can from your present problems, you're thinking positively. So, the idea here is just to not be defeatist. Don't give up so easily—whether your negativity is directed towards you or others. And don't let others give up easily either.

Also, as must be clear from the last exercise, positivity works beautifully when it flows from one person to another. And whomsoever you touch with your positive energy, even if you're still fighting to develop it into a subconscious and integral part of your life, will always be willing to return it to you.

In the end, practicing positivity isn't as hard as falling back into the laziness of negativity. Because the lack of any action, or paralysis of motion, or stagnation of thought and feeling bring about negativity, while active search for joy in the smallest things brings about positivity. You could equate it with being in bed within a darkened bedroom on a beautifully sunny day. Lazing around in bed requires no effort, but brings no joy either. So, step out of the dark confines of your own closed-off mind, step into the sunny brightness of positive warmth, and enjoy your life to the fullest in the beautiful fountain of joy and satisfaction which springs forth.

Finally, I'd like to thank you for purchasing this book! If you enjoyed it or found it helpful, I'd greatly appreciate it if you'd take a moment to leave a review on Amazon. Thank you!

Printed in Great Britain
by Amazon